THE FERRY

between

NEWNHAM *and* ARLINGHAM

Passengers waiting for the ferry, Newnham, *c.* 1920

THE FERRY

between

NEWNHAM *and* ARLINGHAM

MARGARET H. WILLIS

ALAN SUTTON

First Published in the United Kingdom in 1993 by
Alan Sutton Publishing Limited
Phoenix Mill · Far Thrupp · Stroud · Gloucestershire

First Published in the United States of America in 1993 by
Alan Sutton Publishing Inc · 93 Washington Street · Dover · NH 03820

British Library Cataloguing in Publication Data

Willis, Margaret H.
  Ferry: Newnham and Arlingham
  I. Title
  942.413

ISBN 0-7509-0530-1

Typeset in 11/13 Bembo.
Typesetting and origination by
Alan Sutton Publishing Limited.
Printed and bound in Great Britain by
Hartnolls Ltd, Bodmin, Cornwall.

Contents

Foreword

Newnham, with the clock tower, war memorial, fountain, church on the hill and lime trees edging the main street, is an attractive riverside town. It is popular with those who come to the Forest of Dean area, and visitors to the town are pleasantly surprised to be able to walk down Severn Street, formerly Passage Lane, to the river. It was here that, at one time, Newnham had a ferry, which crossed to Arlingham on the opposite bank. It is by the old ferry landing-place that the River Severn, in all its moods, can be seen at close range, although a panoramic view of Horseshoe Bend is visible when standing in the churchyard at the top of the town. Today The Ferry, as the area is commonly called, is a quiet place for a reflective walk or a picnic on the old wall, but in the past it was an important crossing.

Although the life of the passenger ferry between Newnham and Arlingham spanned only a small part of Newnham's history, reference is made in this book to events that took place earlier, where this is necessary to explain the context of a particular occurrence or situation.

In the compilation of information relating to The Ferry, many stories that were gathered were linked to the fishing industry, especially salmon. These have not been included as they are beyond the scope of the book. In answer to questions about The Ferry in its heyday, many memories have been revived, old photographs and letters unearthed and stories retold – the latter have been written down in good faith. The author offers her sincere apologies for any omissions or incorrect statements.

This book does not purport to be a complete study, but simply an attempt to provide a readable account of the happenings at The Ferry before they are completely forgotten.

Margaret Willis
Newnham-on-Severn
Gloucestershire
1993

Acknowledgements

For help and information thanks are expressed to: Ron Aldridge, Barbara Allsopp, the parishes of Arlingham and Awre, Norah Ayland, Vera Beard, Robert G. Bird, The Castle House, Reverend P. Cheeseman (Arlingham), the *Citizen*, H. Cook, Michael L.K. Curtis, J. and N. Elkins, The Gloucester Collection, Gloucester County Records Office, Gloucester Folk Museum, the *Gloucester Journal*, Anita Gould, John Hearn, K.B. Hodgson, Ann Lloyd, the *Mercury*, Phil Morgan, Newnham Library, Newnham School, David Penfold, John Powell, Chris Saunders, Roger Smith, Patrick Turner (Arlingham), B. Wheeler and Brian Willis.

Sincere thanks for the loan of photographs go to: Trevor Askew, Mike Bickerton, Michael Curtis (Arlingham), the family of the late Maurice Fitchett, Dee Huggins, Anita Gould, the executors of Miss J. Kerr's estate, Lesley Leach, Dennis Meek and David Penfold.

The author's fee from the publication of this book is donated to St Peter's church, Newnham-on-Severn, Gloucestershire.

Horses and ferry at Newnham, by E.B. Stanley Montefiore, 1894. (Reproduced by kind permission of Mrs Ellen Pincott, Newnham)

CHAPTER ONE

The Strength of the River Severn

John Leland, writing in the early sixteenth century, noted in his *Itinerary* that 'From Gloucester to Newenham [are] much lowe Groundes, subject to all suddaine Risinge of Severne'. The river often caused great damage, and sometimes the whole of Arlingham was a marsh. Perhaps the river was once narrower between Newnham and Arlingham; Leland certainly wrote of the Severn as 'shallower through "choking sands"'. The historian Thomas Rudge wrote, 'From this town is one of the passages over the river which is perfectly safe, and can be made in almost every state of the tide, for men, horses and carriages', but another historian, Samuel Rudder, wrote, 'Here is a ford, over which at low water wagons and people on horseback, of more reputation than prudence, sometimes pass, for many have lost their lives in the attempt.'

William Fuller came to Newnham in 1813 and afterwards wrote about his visit to Mr John Playsted, with whom he had stayed. His comments about tidal

Newnham from the River Severn. (From an engraving by J. Bonnor)

1

The Severn Bore at Newnham

waves rising 'mountainous high' and turbulent flooding 'which runs with uncommon violence for miles, inundating the lowlands to a vast extent, and foaming and raging like a hideous whirlpool' suggest that the people of Newnham lived in fear of the river. Fuller was probably referring to the famous Severn Bore, which is caused by the progressive constriction of the incoming tide by the increasingly narrow banks and shallow river bed above Sharpness. The tide overcomes the opposing downstream flow of water, thereby causing a standing wave to surge upstream. This bore is at its most spectacular during the high tides of spring and autumn, and gives rise to speculation that the ferry at Newnham could not have been in full-time operation.

Maps dated 1858 show that the form of the river and the distance between the Newnham and Arlingham shores were much the same then as they are today. However, the cliffs at Newnham are still being eroded by both the river and the elements. For example Portland Nab, a cliff near Bullo, is half the size it was half a century ago, when a waterman, Alfred Knight, recalled that at one time 'a hundred people could have danced on the Nab'. From wasteland near the ferry, now part of Brightlands' grounds, a pathway rounded the cliff and led to the lower churchyard, but this is no longer in existence. Although there has been a considerable loss of land on the Newnham side of the river, little has occurred at Arlingham where there are no cliffs to suffer such erosion.

CHAPTER TWO

The Position and Importance
of Newnham

Newnham is thought to have been settled because of the relative ease of traversing the river there. The commanding site, close to the water's edge but above the flood level, was clearly a contributory factor. The crossing at Newnham was presumably in use in the first century AD, and if the ancient line of the road through Arlingham reached the river opposite Hawkins Pill at the north-east corner of Newnham parish, it was presumably to exploit the ford there, which could be used at low water. A stone bench across most of the river bed was connected to the shore by a bar of sand, thus affording a firm passage across.

Historically it is considered that as far back as the Roman invasion the River Severn was crossed between Arlingham and Newnham, for there are traces of a Roman road at Broadoak. Following a battle between the Britons and the Saxons, the Britons, having been defeated at Dyrham, withdrew to

The Severn, Newnham, from Hawkins Pill, *c.* 1920

The fountain, outside The Ship Inn, 1897. There was a chained drinking cup to the left of the fountain, which children enjoyed using. The trough in front of the fountain was for horses but is now used for flowers

the Severn peninsula, close to the important geographical crossing at Newnham. This may account for the local name of Unlawater, for *unla* is the Saxon word for misfortune.

Situated on the bank of the Severn and with easy access from Gloucester, Newnham was once used by royal hunting parties that stayed in the small unnamed Norman castle on the hilltop. Both Henry I and Henry II signed charters at Newnham, and it was from here in 1171 that King Henry II, with Strongbow, Earl of Pembroke, sailed on his expedition to Ireland, landing near Waterford.

In 'By-gone days' (*Arlingham Church and Parish News*, May 1983) Mrs Norah Ayland wrote: 'The Ferry is mentioned in 1238 when King Henry III granted "an oak to the woman keeping the passage at Newnham, so that she could built a boat".' Important ferry rights were often owned by landed gentry or peers of the realm. In the thirteenth century Newnham was a borough returning one member to parliament, but by the fourteenth century The Ferry belonged not to the manor or borough of Newnham but to the lords of the manor of Ruddle in the Westbury Hundred, and this continued until the early part of the nineteenth century.

In the *British Universal Directory* of 1792 for Newnham it is stated that, 'Here is a very safe ferry over the Severn, which is near a mile wide, to Arlingham on the opposite side.'

Newnham bandsmen outside The Ship Inn in front of the fountain, c. 1902. The bandsman on the far left is George Wellington

The Anchor Inn, 1860

Travellers passed through Arlingham in order to cross the River Severn, for here was 'the only place where horse and carriage could ford the river between Gloucester and the sea'. The position of this ford can still be seen at low tide, when the water ripples over the shallow bed of rock a few hundred yards from Newnham, just below Broadoak. In 1802, however, the river's channel changed direction and washed away the bed of sand that joined the rock to the shore. The last person to use this ford was John Smith of Littledean, when he took over the tenancy of Overton Farm, Arlingham, and drove 'his entire stock of cattle and sheep, wagons, goods and family, without loss, over Newnham Passage'. His descendants still farm at Arlingham.

It was, however, because of Newnham's maritime trade and shipbuilding industry, rather than its ferry, that the town became so important after 1700. The River Severn was navigable and tidal, narrowing upstream between Newnham and Arlingham. The position of Newnham at the point where the river widened into a broad estuary, enabling trows to travel up river and brigs down river, made this town the principal port in the area.

Much of Newnham's prosperity therefore depended on river trade and is remembered today by house names such as Mariner's Cottage, Quay House, Ferryside Cottage, Middlewatch House, Ship House and The Ship Inn, which is still trading. The Anchor Inn, which was built in 1710, has now

The clock tower, Newnham, April 1898. The tower, which was erected by public subscription in 1873, was built in stone and is 60 feet high. At this time it had a weather vane

been demolished. Fine houses were built as the town grew, and other industries, in addition to the maritime trade, prospered, such as the tannery and glassworks, and the transport of forest coal. The glassworks was situated near to the old quay, which was built in 1807 near Newnham Pill. It was the first factory in the country to make glass using coal as fuel. Still to be seen today at the old quay are houses thought to be built partly from blocks of refuse from the glassworks, but ongoing research is expected to prove them to be made from iron residue: there were ironworks at Lydney, Cinderford and Parkend, and at Soudley until 1900.

Newnham's importance lessened after 1836, especially with the opening of the Gloucester and Sharpness Canal in 1827 (also known as the Gloucester and Berkeley Canal), when Sharpness became the gateway to the West Midlands and the south-west entrance to the growing national network of waterways. As trade increased at Bullo Pill this had an effect on Newnham's

Severn Street, formerly Passage Lane, leading to The Ferry, Newnham, *c.* 1920. The sign on the left wall reads: 'Upper George Inn' – now 'The Sanctuary'

St Peter's church, Newnham, *c.* 1920. The sign says: 'Cyclists please ride with caution'

trade. Coal from the forest was taken to Bullo Pill and ferried to Gloucester Docks by *Finis*, which was still loading at Bullo in 1903. The owner and captain was Fred Wood from Rodley, who was actually a farmer. The harbour master at Bullo Pill in 1910 was James Ferris.

The railway came to Newnham in 1852, and on summer days in later years people from Cinderford came by train to the 'seaside' sands at The Ferry. In 1910 there were tea-gardens at Quay Cottage. Cattle from Arlingham were ferried to the railway until around 1914.

There had been market fairs at Newnham, customarily held on the feasts of Saints Barnabas and Luke (11 June and 18 October). Pleasure fairs continued up to 1928, with a roundabout and helter-skelter as attractions at the top of the town, outside Victoria Hotel. There was a stretch of water on the Arlingham side of the river, opposite Newnham, known as Victoria Channel, leading to the 'Stype', which was another stretch, near Garden Cliff. Victoria Channel is not, however, considered to be the reason that Victoria Hotel is so named, even though the hotel predates the Victorian era.

There are many well–documented facts about the vessels and channels of water used by skippers at the peak of Newnham's river trade, which reflect the town's prosperity. There are, however, few details relating to ferry legislation or safety. In Henry VIII's reign ferries were subject to old laws that were intended to prevent their misuse: people who kept ferries at Aust,

Broad Oak, near Newnham, c. 1928, The White Hart is on the right

Newnham and other places, and who conveyed horses, cattle or oxen, were forbidden to operate before sunrise or after sunset, or they would be 'liable to fine or imprisonment for infringement'. Part of the Act of Union in 1536, under the guidance of Bishop Rowland Lee, was to regulate the ferries crossing the Severn Estuary and to 'limit their sailing to the hours of daylight'. There was a further Act in the twenty-third year of George III's reign for amending and widening the 'Road from the Passage or Ferry over the River Severn at Newnham, to a Place called Saint Whites, adjoining the Forest of Dean, in the County of Gloucester', mentioning that the road must be kept in good repair past The Bear Inn and the Upper George Inn. The toll for horses, mules, or four-wheeled carriages was 6d; for a drove of oxen 'the sum of 1 shilling and eightpence per score'.

CHAPTER THREE

Early Days

Apart from old engravings, few early pictures of Newnham seen from the Arlingham shore exist. However, the picture below, dating from the eighteenth century, shows the old Passage House, also known as The Bear Inn, on the far left, with an open view to the river and ferry crossing. The picture was catalogued in the late Miss Joan Kerr's estate as follows:

James Holl
Newnham
Signed 'James Holl *delin.*, drawn from the real place'.
Pen and Ink and Grey Wash, on paper, 13¼ x 18½ ins.
Inscribed with a further title on original mount

Newnham. The old Passage House and Passage Lane are on the left

Passage Lane, looking towards the High Street, Newnham

'Newnham in Gloucestershire is a pleasant village near the Forrest of Dean, where there is a Ferry to cross the River Severn – the letter A represents the Ferry or Passage House'

It has been considered that the large pile on the quay to the right of the picture is bark from the forest used in the tanning process. There was a tannery at Broadoak and another at Collow, near Underhill Farm.

In Newnham, two-thirds of the way up the High Street, the street forms a crossroads with the road west to Littledean and Passage Lane. This was recorded in 1594 and leads east to the ferry at Passage Green, which was noted in 1457.

Water Lane and Hormon Lane, mentioned in around 1230, were apparently lanes lying east of High Street towards the river. One of them may have been Back Street, which linked Newnham Pill with the east end of Passage Lane and continued to the church, via Church Street. By 1968 Back Street and Church Street had been renamed Church Road, and Passage Lane was called Severn Street.

CHAPTER FOUR

Newnham Ferry

The ferry as a paying passenger concern began in 1802, when the shifting sands just above Newnham towards Broadoak and the changes in the river channels meant that there was no place to cross to and from Arlingham.

By 1810 the rights in The Ferry had been acquired by the Severn Tunnel Company. According to the *Gloucester Journal* of 19 August 1837 The Bear Inn was offered for sale, together with The Ferry and a fishery, when it was the only posting-house in the town. On 15 July 1843 the same publication carried an advertisement for the 'Sale of The Ferry and Fisheries'. According to *Slater's Directory* there was a Newnham Ferry Co. Ltd. in 1868 owned by The Severn Bank Hotel, but on 3 July 1869 the *Gloucester Journal* carried an advertisement for a sale, on 27 July, of 'Lot I – the Severn Bank Hotel', 'Lot 2 – The Old Bear Hotel' and 'Lot 3 – The Ferry'. At that time the ferry was let

Newnham Ferry, *c.* 1898

Lower High Street, Newnham, before 1905. Preece, the outfitters, is on the right

at £35 a year to Mr Charles Vale of Newnham. The Severn Bank Hotel and The Bear Inn did not reach their reserve.

On 18 December 1869 the *Gloucester Journal* carried an advertisement for the sale of The Bear Hotel, this time without reserve, as a private residence. It is assumed that The Ferry rights were sold prior to the sale. The Severn Bank Hotel was later sold and became a private residence known as Riverdale. It is now the preparatory school, Brightlands, which was opened in 1908.

Henry Preece, a member of the Urban District Council, who had a gent's outfitters where the delicatessen in Newnham is today, owned The Ferry in 1902. He still owned it in 1906, but by 1910 the owners were Tolls Ltd, with Walter Cadogan as the fishery lessee.

Riverdale, Newnham, from the Severn, *c.* 1890

Mr Enoch Williams, founder of the Old Passage Severn Ferry Company, bought The Ferry rights from the London Ferry Company sometime between 1947 or 1948. The ferry survived until after the Second World War when it gradually went out of use.

In the 1970s Mr Horace Cook of Minsterworth bought the ferry and foreshore between Newnham and Arlingham, including the hut on the slipway, by auction at Victoria Hotel from John Williams of Chepstow, the son of Enoch Williams, and he still owns it today.

CHAPTER FIVE

Fisheries

The sale advertisement for The Ferry at Newnham in 1843 was linked with the sale of the 'fisheries'. There was general confusion over the precise meaning of the different kinds of fisheries, but English Law around 1873 divided them into four kinds:

1 A Several fishery, pertaining to a non-navigable river.
2 A Free fishery, concerning an exclusive right of fishing, as in tidal, navigable rivers.

The Castle House, Newnham. This was the home of Maurice Frederic Carter, who was born on 8 April 1826 and was a solicitor from 1848 to 1907. He was also the coroner for the Forest Division of the county from 1868 to 1907. Maurice died on 25 March 1907. His son, Maurice Frederic Carter, and grandson, Maurice Fitzgerald Carter, are buried with him in Newnham churchyard

The ferry, with the trow, *Finis*, rounding The Nab. Percy (left), Tom (centre) and Bert Phillips are in the horse boat. *Finis* was built at Brimscombe in 1881 and was 27 tons in weight. It was travelling up river to the tar works at Gloucester having been loaded with coal from Bullo Pill Dock, and was assisted by a tow boat rowed by two men

3 A Common fishery, either several or free.

4 A Common fishery or Public fishery, where all Queen's subjects are entitled to fish . . . which is generally the case in all tidal waters and navigable rivers.

Following the Salmon Fishery Act of 1873, boards of conservators were given guidance by the Home Office. Of interest to Newnham residents is the twenty-eighth Annual Report of the Severn Fishery Board for 1894, which included a list of conservators and gives the name of the chairman of the sub-district committee for Gloucestershire as Maynard Willoughby Colchester-Wemyss, Esq., who was also vice-chairman of the board, the chairman being J.W. Willis Bund. Included in the elected members of the Severn Fishery Board for the county of Gloucestershire were Maurice Frederic Carter, Gentleman, Newnham, and Russell James Kerr, Esq., The Haie, Newnham. They both attended the meeting of the Board of Conservators of the Severn Fishery District held at the Shirehall, Hereford, on Thursday 17 January 1895, when the 1894 report was presented to the board.

This reference to fisheries, the Severn Fishery Board and its members for 1895 has been included to show that Mr Carter, who was an executive

Newnham, from the river. Tom Phillips, ferryman, is the man wearing waders and standing in the river. The man in the boat wearing a straw hat is a local, Mr Thomas Wicks. The short steps were used by passengers to get onto the ferryman's back before being carried to the boat

member as well as being on the Pollution Committee, was well versed in river law, and well able as a Newnham solicitor to deal with an incident that occurred in 1896. Correspondence in June of that year between Mr Henry Preece, a UDC member, of Newnham and Captain E. Venner of The Reddings, Stonehouse, Arlingham, unfortunately incomplete, highlights a supposed infringement of The Ferry rights, and the matter was put in the hands of Mr Carter, solicitor, of The Castle House (formerly Banksian House), Newnham (outcome unknown). A reference in the letter to 'improvements' corresponds with an article in the *Mercury* dated 29 May 1896, which stated that

> an unusually large number of pleasure seekers came to Newnham on Whit Monday. No less than 1000 persons crossed on The Ferry during the day. No doubt the recent improvements gave impetus to traffic, and several extra men and boats were employed.

CHAPTER SIX

Ferry Rights and Oxen Money

On 8 June 1896 Mr Henry Preece wrote to Captain E. Venner:

Sir,
I am in receipt of your letter of the 3rd inst., respecting the Newnham Ferry.

If you have any documentary evidence of any kind relating to the subject of your letter I shall be very glad to have an opportunity of seeing it, for I quite wish to do what is right and just.

Custom or immemorial usage alone cannot perpetuate a right to usage in a case where profit is essential to its maintenance.

The recently printed table of tolls are calculated so as to enable The Ferry owner to maintain the approaches to the boats in reasonable repair, and efficient boats for the comfort and safety of the persons using The Ferry.

The oxen money paid is about 27/– pr an – less than 6 ½d pr week – it takes so much time and trouble to collect that it is hardly worth doing and as any householder in Arlingham can pay this to The Ferryman or collector at The Ferry at any time, there is surely no hardship in their doing so when they want to cross over.

I cannot assent to the idea that any should go at half price unless the oxen money be first duly paid – please note here the unfairness of the Arlingham people in this matter – only those who require the frequent use of The Ferry pay the 'oxen dues' while the majority refuse to pay. This injustice must be removed if the concession of the half fare is to continue – I quite agree that where a householder has paid 'oxen money' any member of <u>his family</u> living at home shall be entitled to the privilege of the reduction until the following Easter.

The taking of goods across from Arlingham to points on the Newnham shore other than the slipway if in <u>owners boats</u> may be allowed, but if any boat owner carries another mans goods or produce across for a charge it is beyond all question an infringement of The Ferry Rights, as would be the establishment of a joint or propriatary boat of any kind to be so used –

I am going to considerable expense in improving The Ferry on both sides and in providing efficient and suitable boats both for passengers

Newnham 8th June 1896

Sir,
I am in receipt of your letter of the 3rd inst. respecting the Newnham Ferry –

If you have any documentary evidence of any kind relating to the subject of your letter I shall be very glad to have an opportunity of seeing it, for I quite wish to do what is right and just. –

Custom or immemorial usage alone cannot perpetuate a right to usage in a case where profit is essential to its maintainence –

The recently printed Table of tolls are calculated so as to enable the ferry owner to maintain the approaches to the boats in reasonable repair, and efficient Boats for the comfort and safety of the persons using the ferry –

Correspondence regarding Newnham Ferry, 1896. The first and last pages of the letter from Henry Preece to Captain E. Venner are reproduced here and opposite

on both sides and in providing
efficient and suitable boats, both
for passengers, vehicles, goods and
Cattle, the arlingham people
will get the full benefit of this
without any addition to the
fare –

The use of the wharfs
on hither side – apart from the
ferry business – is strictly —
prohibited, and users will be
treated as trespassers to be dealt
with as the High Court of Justice
determine —

I am

Sir

Yours faithfully,

Henry Reece.

E. E. S. Vennill Esq.
The Reddings,
Stonehouse,
Glo;

21

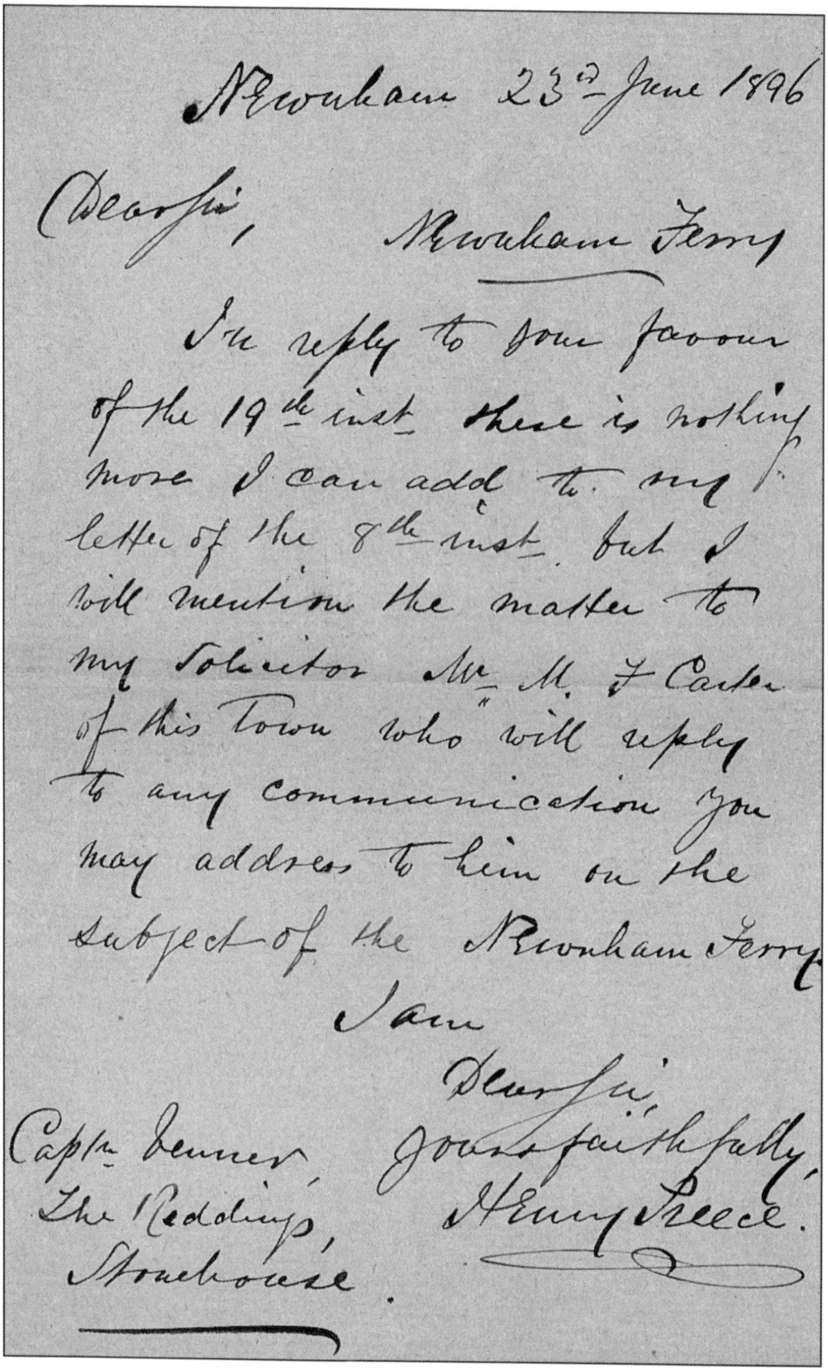

Newnham 23rd June 1896

Dear Sir, Newnham Ferry

In reply to your favour of the 19th inst there is nothing more I can add to my letter of the 8th inst. but I will mention the matter to my Solicitor Mr M. F Carter of this Town who will reply to any communication you may address to him on the subject of the Newnham Ferry

I am

Dear Sir,

Yours faithfully,

Henry Reece.

Capt. Venner,
The Reddings,
Stonehouse.

A letter to Captain E. Venner

The Ferry, Newnham, *c.* 1900

vehicles, goods and cattle. The Arlingham people will get the full benefit of this without any addition to the fare.

The use of the wharf on hither site – apart from The Ferry business – is strictly prohibited and users will be treated as trespassers to be dealt with as the High Court of Justice determine.

I am Sir Yours faithfully

Henry Preece

Captain Venner replied to this letter on 19 June, following which Mr Preece asked his solicitor, Mr M.F. Carter of Newnham, to reply to 'any communication you may address to him on the subject of the Newnham Ferry'.

Two further letters from Captain Venner, dated 24 and 25 June 1896, refer to interviews with 'Mr. Wintle as agreed when at the last meeting of the P. Council', and later 'I think on second thoughts it would be well to consult Mr. Sayer before taking further steps about The Ferry . . . will you please therefore copy roughly the letters of Mr. Preece and also mine . . . to show to Mr. Wintle when we consult him, also to the County Council.'

There are no details about the final outcome, but the oxen money was still a matter of dispute in 1921.

CHAPTER SEVEN

Ferry Fares

On 2 May 1921 the Arlingham Parish Council had an item on the agenda of the meeting to 'discuss matters relating to The Ferry'. The following are some of the statements taken, recorded in a solicitor's notebook (presumably that of Mr Carter):

Mr. Hy Smith states re the Oxen money for crossing The Ferry at half rate as follows: 'I am 67 years of age. As long as my rememberance this Oxen has been paid yearly at Easter. Until quite recently, there has been an house to house collection. Until Mr. Preece came in possession, the full fare was 3d (less than five pence today) there and back. Half price to the Oxen payers.'

Mr. Albert Fryer states that he is now 73 years of age, and was born at The Red Lion, in Arlingham parish, and all the years that he lived in the

The Ferry, *c.* 1929

The butchers, previously The Lamb and Flag Inn, Newnham, *c.* 1903

parish he paid Oxen money, and his father before him. His father died at the age of 84 years and have now been dead 60 years as he was only 13 years old when his father died, and this has always been called for at the house and we never paid more than 1½d there and back. I crossed The Ferry daily to go to a school at Broadoak. I have always heard that it was half price for all goods or anything the oxen payers sent over the river. (Dated and signed as a true statement 2.5.1921.) A. Fryer.

Thos. Butt statement re the Oxen money 'He is now over 70 years of age. He had always heard that the Arlingham people were entitled to cross The Ferry by paying Oxen at half fare and the charge so long as he could remember was 3d there and back, and half price, if they paid the Oxen'.

Miss. Elizabeth Hayward states that her father worked The Ferry and rented the Rights for many years and her grandfather before that and she had many times heard him say that the Arlingham people could put in an extra boat this side, so the Arlingham people made arrangements with The Ferry owners to be put across with goods, etc. at half fare, with a yearly subscription being collected at Easter as an acknowledgement and which was called Oxen. Robert Hayward says he was Ferryman for eight years when his father rented it, about 40 years ago, as he is now 72 years of age. During that time he always went round at Easter from house to house and collected this Oxen money.

The farmers which paid most was charged 2/6d, Tradesmen 1/6d, small cottagers as low as 6d. If they did not pay they were charged the full price of threepence. This entitled people to cross over or send anything they liked, at half fare. There was never any variation of the charges since he can remember. He think this priviledge was granted for giving the owners a free landing on our Manor.

An interesting statement in the same set of papers, dated 2 May 1921, is as follows:

NEWNHAM PASSAGE RE OXEN

I beg to relate that my father was continually crossing over the river by The Ferry boat and was paying 1½d double journey for himself and the same price for what he was sending, my paying the Oxen 1/6d per year. On my own account, I am now 82 years of age and have traded backward and forwards nearly every day between 1865 and 1894 and was not asked to pay more than the ordinary fare which was the same as the above. The Oxen I paid was 2/6d per year. I traded as butcher between those dates and sent the meat hampers and always paid the ordinary fare 1 ½d each and Hides the same.

I can remember the farmers some of them sending their wheat accross The Ferry to Mill at Lydney and that was at half price by paying 2/6d Oxen.

The Stroud Brewery formerly sent their beer across The Ferry before the G.W.R. ran two or three wagonloads at a time.

Signed: [The name is hard to decipher, but is considered to be Ira B. Vernon – there was a Vernon Family in Arlingham.]

CHAPTER EIGHT

The Ferrymen

The best-remembered ferryman was Mr Tom Phillips. Parish registers and census returns record the following:

Baptism–'William Thomas Phillips, son of Mary Ann Phillips, baptised at Arlingham, 3rd January, 1858.'
1871 census – listed as 'William T. Phillips, age 13, in household of grandfather Richard Phillips (waterman) and his wife Mary.'
1881 census – 'at Burnham-on-Sea, Somerset: Thos. Phillips, able seaman, age 21, single, born at Arlingham; crew member of the *Ocean Child*, a 42 ton ketch carrying between Lydney and Bridgewater.'

Tom Phillips approaching the slipway, *c.* 1929

Tom Phillips was born on 2 September 1857. He was brought up by his grandparents, Richard and Mary Phillips. His mother eventually married John Dangerfield on 26 December 1865. Tom married Fanny Hayward on 2 December 1885 at St Michael's church, Gloucester.

Tom and Fanny first lived in Arlingham, then moved to a cottage in Broadoak, afterwards to a house in Preece's Entry, Newnham, and then finally, between 1907 and 1908, to a house at Undercliffe, where they lived for the rest of their lives. In fact there were two houses at Undercliffe, and because of the size of their family (they had fifteen children) they ended up occupying both of them. These houses have now been demolished because the river bank started to erode and there was a danger of the houses falling into the Severn. Some of the children were brought up by relatives. For example, Agnes Mary, who was born 16 May 1889 and baptized at Arlingham, and her younger sister May, who was born 10 February 1896 (who later married John Meadows), went to live with childless relations at the Lea Bailey.

Tom Phillips worked for the owner of the ferry for thirty–seven years and used a wooden hut near the ferry as a shelter, to store fish and to cobble shoes when he was not busy. The hut had a small side window, which local residents believe was used for the payment of ferry monies, and there was a

The Severn, *c*. 1910. Undercliffe House (left), the home of Tom Phillips, is now demolished

St Peter's church, Newnham, *c.* 1896

lifebelt on a side wall. Tom was known to swill down the cobblestones at The Ferry area so as to keep it clean for people using the ferry.

One of Tom's sons, Bertram David, who was baptized on 2 February 1898, married Mary Beatrice Pearsall. Their daughter Megan lived at Undercliffe Cottage until she was twelve years of age, when the family moved to Severn Street. She later married John Lusty, and they still live in the same cottage in Severn Street, which at one time was used as the local telephone exchange. One of Tom's daughters, Violet Olive, who was born on 3 May 1886 and baptized at Arlingham on 29 August 1886, married Alfred Jesse Brobyn and had two sons, Gaius and Donald. Gaius was best man at the marriage between Ann and Dennis Lloyd of Newnham in 1948.

There are many reminiscenses of Tom in *Recollections of Arlingham from 1916 to the Early 1920s*. The author, Mrs Lucy Mitchell (née Greenway), wrote:

We lived on the other side of the Severn, the only access to and from our home being ferried across. Then passengers would shout for Tom Phillips to come and oblige. This he would do if he felt like it! He was not a big

St Peter's church and The Ferry, Newnham, from the Severn

man, but he would lift quite weighty people from the boat and carry them the short distance through 'dear old Severn mud' to terra firma!

A letter was published in the *Arlingham Church and Parish News* in April 1983, written by Bert Hayward of Weobley, Herefordshire. An extract reads:

The alternative way in which we used to reach Arlingham was by train to Newnham-on-Severn, as it was always known in olden days, and then over The Ferry. This was run by Tom Phillips who wore long leather thigh-boots and who looked an awesome figure to a small boy. If the tide was high it was a case of from bank to bank, but low tides were a very different matter. He had a series of planks secured into the sand, and very narrow they were. I remember on one occasion my mother missed her footing and sunk one leg into the mud. She was never all that fond of Arlingham and this did little to improve it. I recall that at one time Tom had a lug-sail to help him, on which in large letters was an advertisement for Beecham's Pills. When not ferrying, he would sit in his hut and repair shoes.

Rosa Ayland (1894–1985), the daughter of Arthur and Sarah Jane Cave-Ayland of Arlingham, wrote in the same publication in February 1983 of her

The wedding of Tom Phillips's daughter Muriel (known as Ginny) and Fred Frewen. The bearded man sitting on the right is Tom Phillips and Fanny, his wife, is next to him. Behind them are their sons Bert (back row, far right), Percy (left) and Edgar (right). In front of the bridge, either side of the dog, are Gaius (left) and Donald (right) Brobyn. The vicar is the Revd Fasson of St Peter's church, Newnham, and the lady to his right is Violet Hayward (later Mrs Trevor Askew), the daughter of another ferryman, Bill Hayward

memories of Arlingham. She recalls the headmaster of Arlingham School wearing his cap and gown on particular national occasions, for example, when he announced to the school the end of the Boer War, the death of Queen Victoria, the coronation of Edward VII and so on. These important communications were brought to the school by a pupil who lived at the pub at The Passage, where the news had been brought by The Ferryman, 'Old Tom Phillips', who had himself received it from the postmistress at Newnham.

On 3 November 1927 the *Citizen* newspaper carried the following article:

NEWNHAM FERRYMAN

FOR 37 YEARS

PRESENTATION TO MR. W.T. PHILLIPS

Henry and Rosa Bevis at the front door of Arlingham vicarage on the occasion of their Golden Wedding Anniversary, 5 June 1928. The Revd Henry Bevis was vicar of Arlingham for forty-one years, from April 1893 to December 1934. He was born at Ramsgate in 1842, the son of the Revd Henry Joseph Bevis, and was educated at Morden Hall, Surrey, Cheshunt College and Christ's College, Cambridge. He died on 14 December 1936 and was buried in Arlingham churchyard (Photograph: Mr Peter Randford, Arlingham)

The parishioners of Arlingham called a special meeting at the Infants' School when Mr. William Thomas Phillips, for 37 years The Ferryman at Newnham, who recently retired, was presented with a purse of money as a token of appreciation of the faithful service rendered in conveying passengers across The Ferry from Newnham to Arlingham.

Mrs. Bevis, wife of the Rev. H. Bevis (Vicar of Arlingham) in making the presentation, spoke of the cheerful and kindly way in which Mr. Phillips had carried out his duties and wished him on behalf of the parishioners of Arlingham, many years of good health and happiness in his retirement.

Mr. Phillips replied, and in thanking the donors, said it was a great pleasure to him to have had the invitation to the school which he attended 63 years ago, and still a greater pleasure to know that he had given satisfaction in his work.

Tom Phillips retired in 1927 and died on 14 February 1939, aged eighty-one. Fanny died on 12 October 1949, aged eighty-five. They are both buried in Newnham churchyard.

Tom was succeeded as ferryman by his stepson, William 'Bill' Hayward. William was baptized on 20 March 1884 at Arlingham. In 1907 Bill worked in a temporary capacity on building The Bay at Newnham Station, as part of the gangers and sub-gangers team from Bullo, under Inspector Trotman. Bill then went to Tredegar and was working in the pits in around 1925. In 1926 Bill and his wife, Martha Ellen, came back to Newnham with their daughter, Violet, and lived in a cottage at Bullo next to Trevor Askew's home. Trevor was born in Hereford in 1907 and had come to Newnham as a babe in arms.

Violet worked at The Castle House as nursemaid to Fitzgerald, Tracey and Richard Carter, walking to and from Bullo each morning and evening. Trevor got to know her and sometimes walked with her. When he was twenty-two he and Violet married. The ceremony took place on 16 December 1932 at St Peter's church, Newnham, with Reverend Dodd officiating.

Bill Hayward and his wife moved to Ferryside Cottage, which was once part of the stables belonging to The Bear Inn. Trevor and Violet lived with them there, together with their own daughter, Veronica.

Trevor occasionally helped his father-in-law, Bill, with The Ferry at weekends and even carried people over himself. The fare was 6d one way and 9d for one person and a bicycle. Cycling clubs used to write to Bill to say how many members would be going over the river on the ferry, and the number of boats was adjusted accordingly. Sometimes bicycles were taken in one boat and people in another.

Bill Hayward always carried a big pair of binoculars in order to see people on the Arlingham side. He is also remembered for befriending a stray ginger and white cat, which had double front paws and lived at the hut. It was fed on bread and milk, and scraps from people using the ferry. Bill died, aged sixty-five, in November 1948 and his wife died, aged sixty, in April 1949. They are both buried in Newnham churchyard. Trevor and Violet continued to live at Ferryside Cottage until 1958.

The shelter for the ferryman was on the Newnham side of the river so that it was easy for passengers to locate him. At Arlingham, however, people had to go down the bank to call to The Ferryman. As there was so much mud on the Arlingham side, passengers timed their passage for high water.

Writing in 1947, Brian Waters stated in *Severn Tide* that:

those living in Newnham and Arlingham make little use of The Ferry. The Ferryman who sometimes does not have a passenger for days, spends his

William (Bill) Hayward and his wife, Martha Ellen, *c.* 1925

Bill Hayward carrying a passenger ashore at
Arlingham Passage, *c.* 1930

time cobbling shoes, so that often the call of the traveller fails to rouse him
from his last . . . as he rows towards you, you know that there is no
escaping him. He answers your good day but he regards you not as a fellow
human being, but as cargo. No matter what you weigh . . . he hoists you
on to his shoulders and before you can diffidently protest about your
weight he has carried you through the shallows and dumped you in his
boat.

The ferryman was considered to be a kindly man who often kept
passengers waiting while he was giving children a pleasure ride. In 1965
Leonard Clark recalled in *A Fool in the Forest* that when he was ten

there was a man, a retired boat builder, who used to ferry people over . . .
from the Newnham bank to the mud flats on the other side. Everybody
knew how treacherous and strong were the currents in that spot and how
necessary it was for the right time of day to be chosen for the crossing.

On one day in particular, Clark and a friend wanted to take the ferry to
Arlingham. As it was low tide they decided to wait until the tide was right, at

St Peter's church, Newnham, from the Severn, *c.* 1920

which point they were carried in turn in the ferryman's arms over the mud. When the children wanted to return to Newnham in the evening they could not make the ferryman hear, despite calling many times. Despondently thinking of home, they were joined by a woman who told them that he would probably be in The Sailor. Singing was heard and the ferryman at last turned up, but he was not in a happy mood, referring to them as 'boys who should be in bed at that time of night'. With an increasing wind the boat was rocked from side to side, and it became clear that the ferryman had missed the proper channel and was incapable of rowing against the tide. As a result the boat moved downstream. After a frightening journey, during which it started to rain, the children reached the Newnham shore over a mile from the town and had a long walk home. When well on their way they realized that they had not paid for the ride!

Violet Phillips, later Violet Brobyn, kept a ledger of all the passengers and goods dealt with on the ferry, first for Tom Phillips and then for Bill Hayward. She gave this ledger to Mr Enoch Williams when he bought the ferry, and in it she wrote that the greatest number of passengers on one day was 1,013, which confirms the *Mercury* article dated May 1896 (see p. 18).

William Bodnum married Hannah Aldridge at Arlingham in 1829. They had eight children, the last of whom was Sarah Ann, baptized at Arlingham in 1844. Sarah Ann married William Smith (born in Newnham in 1840) in Gloucester in 1862. It is widely considered that they deliberately married at St Nicholas's church in Westgate Street, Gloucester, either to avoid offending one or other of their families (who may have wished them to be married at Newnham or Arlingham), or to avoid the problems of Sarah Ann having to

Bill Hayward and Mrs Wilkinson, the
daughter of a former vicar of
Arlingham, the Revd Thomas
Ravenhill, on the shore of the Severn,
April 1933

cross the Severn in a small ferry boat wearing a wedding dress! It is
impossible to tell when William Bodnum became a ferryman on the
Newnham–Arlingham ferry or when he moved to Newnham, but the latter
was presumably after his marriage in 1829.

In the 1861 census William was reported as residing at Passage Lane,
Newnham, and having the occupation of 'waterman'. At Sarah Ann's
marriage in 1862 his occupation was described as 'ferryman'. In the 1871
census he is recorded as living with his son-in-law at Newnham Street,
Newnham. He would have been sixty-six at this time. He died in 1881 aged
seventy-six and was buried at Arlingham.

Records show that other ferrymen included the following:

Thomas Knight of Newnham, ferryman in around 1809;

Lewis Hayward, listed as 'ferryman' in the 1881 census at the age of
twenty-six, and born at Arlingham. He was the son of Samuel Hayward, an
innkeeper;

Samuel Hayward, recorded as 'ferryman' in 1885 in *Kelly's Directory for
Newnham*;

John Dee, also listed as 'ferryman' in 1889 in *Kelly's Directory for Newnham*;

Harry Aldridge of Greenhaye Cottages, High Street, Arlingham.

CHAPTER NINE

The Ferry Users

Mr D. Meadows, the son of Esther Annie Tugwell (born in 1884 and buried in Cardiff), talks of Passage Row. This was perhaps a former local name given to the cottages on the left-hand side of Passage Lane, which adjoin the gardens of the Upper George Inn, now The Sanctuary. There were no cottages on the right-hand side until after 1860, the land having previously been owned by The Bear Inn. There is no Passage Row at Arlingham, but there is a Passage Road.

The importance of the ferry to the people of Arlingham increased in the 1890s, when they could cross the river and catch a train to South Wales to look for work. Three sons of the builder Thomas Greenway went to Newport and opened businesses there. One had an outfitters and two were master builders.

Mr Hirom, whose sons Eddie and Rochford became local builders, had a bakery on The Green at Newnham in 1908 and went over to Arlingham on the ferry to trade, bringing back cream and farm produce. The present owner of his cottage, Dave Cullis, found a bread oven in good condition during renovation work. It was complete with old Hovis tins and large trays to draw out the bread. These items are now in the Dean Heritage Museum.

In the book *Brightlands* Glyn Hardwicke states that

Across the Severn from Newnham stands Arlingham where, in 1910, Sir Lionel Darrell ran a pack of beagles. Occasionally a party of boys from Brightlands were ferried across the river by a local character named 'Old Tom', in his boat with a red sail bearing the legend 'Beechams Pills'. They would be welcomed by Sir Lionel with an invitation to follow his precious animals. This they did for 8–10 miles.

As a favour a gentleman who lived at The Bear Inn, Mr Thomas Weeks, used to ferry people across the river to Arlingham, in either a sailing or a rowing-boat, to bathe on the sands at Arlingham. The Bear Inn was once the place where petty sessions were held and travellers changed horses, with the animals and grooms staying in stables. Today the stables are cottages, known as Ferryside, in an unmade lane (passage) that leads to The Ferry. The Bear Inn is at present undergoing renovation work and has been renamed The Passage

A passenger being carried to the ferry from the Arlingham side of the Severn, *c.* 1902

House again. It is situated at the end of Passage Lane, which was once the main trade route from the Forest of Dean.

In 1913 Arthur Cooke wrote in *The Forest of Dean*:

> To those who have the time and will to leave the Forest for a while and cross the Severn stream, a ferry at the bottom of a cross street of the town offers the way. At low tide a small portion only of the journey will be made by boat; the remaining area of tenacious mud-flats stretching from the farther shore must needs be traversed in The Ferryman's strong arms.

In around 1920 Mrs Alice Wyman and Mrs Doris White (whose daughter Phyllis became the wife of the late Fred Burcher of Newnham) lived in the cottages on the lane leading to The Ferry and used to take out trays of tea to sell to people who came to picnic there.

In 'Arlingham remembered', an article in a booklet published by the Village Appraisal Committee in 1991, it is stated that in 1921 the means of transport to Gloucester was by horse and trap, by horse-drawn village carrier or by ferry across the river to Newnham railway station.

Newnham Ferry was considered by Charles Wellington to be primitive. In November 1927 he wrote an article entitled 'A strange ferry' for the *Austin* magazine, a copy of which is in Gloucester Library. It was reprinted in the *Arlingham Church and Parish News* in February 1989:

St Peter's church (centre), The Castle House (left) and the chimneys of Brightlands (right), from Bullo Fields, Newnham, *c.* 1910

Halfway up the Severn there is a weird and primitive ferry, which is worth a visit if only for the thrills incidental to its working.

Approaching this ferry from the Gloucester and Bristol side you will have to drive through a strange district, very aloof from the world . . . and forthwith you will arrive by way of quaint little lanes, and very suddenly, at the broad open flow of the Severn, with Newnham Church and its clustering groups of houses, capping the blood-red cliff opposite. Perhaps Newnham bells will be pealing, and very pleasant they are, heard across the water. Here one must leave the car, and The Ferryman (who is usually on the opposite side of the river) pulls across.

The voyage over the Severn is easy enough, and it is good to explore this quaint little town, with its air of aloof gentility, and its strange melange of sea-faring, salmon-fishing folk, with an upper stratum one would expect to meet in . . . novels. Then there is the churchyard, beautifully situated, overlooking the great expanse of pink and golden sand, on which at low tide, great flocks of water fowl find entertainment, food and lodgement . . .

But, the quiet excitements of Newnham-on-Severn exhausted, we have to cross the river once more to get to our car: by this time the tide has come up in great style from the Bristol Channel, and the sturdy boatman has something to do to stem the flow. He makes a zig-zag course, however, and gets across to a point about fifty yards from the bank . . .

Tom Phillips with a ferryload of passengers, ready to leave Arlingham Passage for Newnham, *c.* 1912. (Postcard from Gloucester Library)

And now for the excitement: Old Charon – in Ancient Legend Charon is forever ferrying passengers over the Styx – as the frivolous lady of the party christens him – puts on an enormous pair of wading boots, and breaks the news gently that – from this point – we must be carried ashore; the water is too shallow to take the boat in further! And so – greatly to the delight of a select and appreciative audience of children from the farmhouse on the bank – we are, one after the other, hoisted on to Charon's broad shoulders – pick-a-back style – and transported by manpower to the bank!

He was a sturdy fellow, this Charon, for one or two of us tipped the scale at 12 or 14 stone, and he did his work well! But . . . pick-a-back travelling is not elegant, one does not know what to do with one's legs.

Still, we all arrived safely and dry shod, and we left for home, speculating whether there could be a more arduous undertaking than that of poor old Charon, and wondering what would happen if we had brought along some worthy of 'great' weight – but perhaps there is a weight limit at Newnham Ferry!

Newnham from the church tower. The Victoria Hotel is on the left and the Armoury Hall is just left of centre in the background

Mr Ewart Wood, known as 'Tom', was a blacksmith. He lived at The Ruffitt but was born at Ruspidge. In the 1920s he used the ferry to take his bicycle across to Arlingham, then cycle to Reading to court his future wife, who was in service there. When Tom finally retired he had a blacksmith's shop under the bridge at Worcester Street, Gloucester, where he worked on Saturday mornings.

Again in the 1920s Elizabeth Hyett, formerly of Rodley and now at Staunton, remembers taking a picnic tea to the sands near The Ferry at Newnham. She arrived by pony and trap, driven by her father, Frank Hyett, of Hutts Farm.

Dr and Mrs Selby, both now deceased, came to Newnham in 1928. Their daughter, Margaret, recalls being taken, at the age of six, with her brother and sister plus bicycles, over on the ferry to Arlingham and being carried over the mud by the ferryman. They had to wait for the tide to turn before they could return.

Helter-skelter and merry-go-round outside Victoria Hotel, *c.* 1925. Fryer (left) was the stationer, bookseller and music seller. The board to the right is a sign for The Kings's Head Inn

A merry-go-round at Newnham, *c.* 1925

Nesta Fryer, who was born in 1913 and still lives at Etloe, vividly remembers the carefulness with which, in about 1928, the ferryman, clad in oilskins, carried her over the mud to the ferry boat. She and her friend, the late Margaret Morse (the daughter of Mr Charles Morse of Gatcombe, who rented all the fishery between Gatcombe and Wellhead Bay from the Bathurst Park Estate), had decided to take their bicycles to Arlingham on the ferry. They cycled through Arlingham to Sharpness and made the return journey on the old Severn Bridge Railway with their bicycles in the guard's van, the station being about a mile from Etloe. It was this type of train, with two carriages and a guard's van, that took salmon from Lydney to Billingsgate in London.

The good grazing lands at Arlingham are remembered by Cyril Boughton, whose father, Francis, farmed at Church Farm, Littledean. The farmer used to take lambs over on the ferry to fatten them, in preparation for their eventual sale as far away as Whitminster. Although some lambs jumped overboard, not one was lost!

The Armoury Hall in Newnham was built in 1826 and was at one time a local artist's studio. The artist was E.B. Montefiore and he lived at The Old Vicarage in High Street, Newnham. The hall was also once used as a chapel by the Plymouth Brethren, and in the 1940s members of the Brethren in

Arlingham came by ferry to the hall in Newnham for their meetings. In 1962 the hall became a parish hall.

Anita Gould remembers that in the 1930s Bill Hayward used to keep an eye on any children he saw playing on the sands at The Ferry. He would demonstrate the dangers of the river bed, which shelved away suddenly, by stepping sideways, putting up his hand and partly disappearing under the water, to the consternation of the children!

The Foord brothers, Michael and Geoffrey, whose mother still lives at Bullo, had a canoe which they used to paddle over to Arlingham to the flat, sandy mud there. In 1945 Kenneth Pearkes, who had a flat–bottomed rowing-boat, would cross the river to go mushrooming in Arlingham. The late Harold Davis, together with Sonny and Raymond Trigg, also had their own rowing-boats which they used to cross the river.

Peter Warner's father, Tom, who was a farmer and cattle dealer at Awre, was the last man to cross on the ox boat ferry. His horse swam over by the side of the boat to be broken in by Mr Bert King of The New Inn, Arlingham.

David Duval, who lived in Arlingham, attended Brightlands School as a boarder from May 1943 until July 1950. His mother brought him to school on the ferry, and he clearly remembers waving goodbye to her from the top–floor dormitory windows which overlooked the river.

People waiting at The Ferry for the tide – a usual feature on high days and holidays, c. 1920. The building on the right is the old wharf

When Miss Gwynneth Jones, who was born in 1905 and who still lives at Cotswold, Church Road, Newnham, visited Mr and Mrs Watkins at Arlingham, Tom Philips was the ferryman. There was more mud on the Arlingham side and often the ferryman had quite a walk to the shore while carrying his passenger. On arrival there was a further mile's walk through an avenue of walnut trees to get to the village.

The Watkins' son, Harold, worked for J.H. Jones and Co. in Newnham High Street (where the antiques shop is today) and used the ferry to get to work. He stayed in Newnham for the week, taking the ferry back to Arlingham each weekend. His parents later moved to Birmingham.

Frances Knight, née Bluett, recalls sitting in the bottom of the ferry boat which was taking sheep and rams from Culverhouse Farm, previously known as Blythe Court, to a farm at Arlingham. The ferryman at the time was Bill Hayward.

About once a week 'Butcher' Price, of 'Price late Morse' butchers (once the Lamb and Flag inn, known today as Flag House, High Street, Newnham), would use the ferry to go to Arlingham for stock. He also ferried people over the river as a favour.

The parents of Mr K. Hodgson of West Sussex were the master and matron of The Beeches children's home from 1931 to 1947. Hodgson's father was a special constable. On one winter's night in the early 1940s he was called out by Mr Raymond Bennet (chief cashier of Lloyds Bank who lived nearby in Severndene) because a lady was in difficulties in the river by the boathouse, where the salmon nets and boats were kept. His father saved her and was awarded the Royal Humane Society's medal, presented to him by the Lord Lieutenant of the county. The Ferry area was fortunately out of bounds for the twenty-eight children in the home. Hodgson's parents used to go over to Arlingham with their bicycles by ferry, from where they would cycle to Thornbury to visit a home there. The Ferryman carried each of them and their bicycles in turn to the shore.

In the 1940s sheep were brought to Newnham from Arlingham by 'Jock' Morris, father of Christopher Morris of The Green, ferried over by Bill Hayward. The sheep were led up Severn Street to the slaughterhouse behind the premises of 'Butcher' Price, now Flag House. Jock's dog went with them, but used to swim back and, helped by the tide, often landed nearer to Broadoak!

In the 1950s Josie and Richard Beard of Newnham were taken over the river to visit relations in Overton Lane, Arlingham, by Mr Edwin 'Nip' Price – no relation of the butcher – in a rowing-boat. It took about fifteen minutes, and wellington boots were always taken to don before getting off in the mud on the other side at Arlingham Passage. Arrangements were made for the return journey according to the tide.

Unlawater Hotel (centre) and The Beeches (right), *c.* 1930

Newnham station, the scene of many meetings prior to taking the ferry to Arlingham. The railway was also used as a means of transport for Arlingham people going to Gloucester after taking the ferry across the river to Newnham

In the late 1950s Keith Rodgers, who was born in Lydney but lived at Broadoak, when he was not away with the Merchant Navy, used to convey Rambler's Association members across on the ferry for William Hardy, who was the association chairman, as well as the owner of the fishing rights on that stretch of the Severn. The ramblers walked from Littledean to The Ferry, crossed to Arlingham, and walked on the other side to Minsterworth, where they were transported back by the fishermen there.

In the 1960s William 'Buster' Hardy, who worked for the LMS railway (his brother James worked for the GWR), had some boats and sometimes, as a favour, took passengers over to Arlingham, mainly to visit The New Inn, now The Passage Inn. William Hardy obtained the fishing rights of the river between the Horseshoe Bend and Garden Cliff. These have been passed on to his son Christopher, who still lives in Newnham.

Several people recall taking their bicycles over to Arlingham using the ferry. There is a large photograph of a boat full of bicycles, passengers and the ferryman, in a Newnham cottage, which bears this out.

Passage Lane

Many years ago Harry Aldridge of Greenhaye Cottages, Arlingham, used to row people from Arlingham to Newnham as a favour. His father was Captain Lewis Aldridge who owned sailing ships, including *Emily*, a schooner-rigged ketch that traded in coal, sailing out of Lydney to Ireland and the Channel ports, but travelling also to Bullo Pill.

One local resident, who still misses the whistle of Edgar Phillips (the son of Tom Phillips) at The Ferry, recalls people collecting coal and wood from the foreshore at The Ferry area. These are believed to have been spillages from barges, which had been loosened by tides, although there are some who remain convinced that there is actually coal beneath the river bed! Horace Coopy had a winch at the back of his cottage at Broadoak to collect wood floating on the river.

Donald Brobyn, born in Newnham but living in Blakeney, wrote to the *Gloucester Journal* in 1990 when he was about eighty. He thought that few people would be aware that there was a ferry landing-stage, made of pitch and pine, quite near to the resting place of the *Finis* at Arlingham. This was always used for transporting horses and cattle over the river. Most of it is now concealed by mud.

CHAPTER TEN

A Romantic Link

Schooner captain, Hugh Shaw, met Captain Henry Aldridge when their vessels were moored next to each other at Garston, Liverpool, and again some months later when an invitation was extended to Hugh from Henry to visit Arlingham. Norah Ayland recounted the following story in her book *Schooner Captain*:

> he met me at Newnham railway station. Newnham stands on the opposite side of the river from Arlingham and The Ferry on the river is about a mile from the station. Waiting in the ferry boat to take us to the Arlingham shore was the grand old ferryman, Tom Phillips, or 'Old Tom' as he was affectionately called by everyone. I got to know him well later on and became very fond of him.

Newnham station

Tom Phillips at The Ferry, Newnham, *c.* 1920

Hugh thought that Arlingham village, a mile from the river crossing, was a lovely place and received a great welcome from Henry's wife. Henry became 'Harry' to Hugh, and as they had all got on so well Hugh extended his stay by a day, first crossing by ferry again to telephone his agent to find out if he was needed by his loading vessel.

Harry's young sister returned from a holiday that same day and met Hugh, who was instantly attracted to her. When he was due to leave Arlingham he asked her to walk to The Ferry with him. They were there in no time, with nothing being said about meeting each other again. Just before Hugh boarded he asked Harry's sister if she would write to him. Their parting was witnessed by Old Tom, The Ferryman.

They corresponded, and Hugh was invited to spend Christmas at Arlingham, but he decided he could not wait until then (it was now

The Passage Inn, previously The New Inn, Arlingham, from Newnham

September) and wrote to say he would be there the next weekend. He remembered little of the railway journey, and it was only when he came to The Ferry and saw 'Old Tom's face, all smiles, and remembering how he had watched me when I said goodbye to her only a short time ago, that I realised my secret was not my own.' They were married at Arlingham church on 19 January 1910 and had five children.

Captain Hugh Shaw retired from the sea in 1947 and died in 1966.

CHAPTER ELEVEN

Arlingham

Arlingham is a small village at the end of a peninsular of farmland, surrounded on three sides by the River Severn. There is no green and the houses do not cluster around the church. The main occupation in Arlingham is agriculture – the land is fertile – and previously large estates have now been divided into smaller farms. Arlingham still has a village shop, which is well supported.

There is no village school in Arlingham today. The primary school closed in 1984, when the Arlingham children marked its closure by going to Newnham by ferry. Likewise children from Newnham School crossed to Arlingham, though not on the same day. They were ferried by Bill Wayman. The names of Class 4 children who went across the river from Newnham to Arlingham to mark the closure of Arlingham School were:

Sarah Foord	Stuart Handscombe	Timothy Brooks
Rebecca Pattman	Tracy Rodgers	Donrad Caulkett
Jason Nicholas	Jeremy Fraser	Giles Heeks

Newnham Ferry, from Arlingham, *c.* 1929

St Mary's church, Arlingham, *c.* 1896

Kerry Hawkins	Susan O'Connell	Simon Ulyatt
Matthew Kibb	Liajm O'Hara	Caroline Wayman
Lee Evans	Amanda Warder	Helen Gwilliam

St Mary's church was built in 1372 and has changed little over the years. The churchyard quietly reveals the names and homes of one-time residents of Arlingham as well as some from Newnham.

When census records began in 1801, Arlingham's inhabitants numbered 506. This number increased to the highest ever figure of 793 in 1841, owing to increased ship and barge traffic on the river. This in turn brought about the decline of Arlingham's fortunes with the building of the canal linking Sharpness with Gloucester. Ships preferred to use the canal, thus avoiding the meandering river with its tidal complications.

After the Second World War Newnham ferry ceased to operate and links with Arlingham were reduced. In 1991 43 per cent of the parishioners (there were some 148 households) said they would like to see the ferry service re-established.

CHAPTER TWELVE

Arlingham Stories

Mr Patrick Turner, who was born in 1933, went to Arlingham School and still farms at Lower Milton End Farm, Arlingham. His grandfather, Frank Bettridge, who was born in 1860, used to take a pony and trap down to The Ferry to pick up Mr Jordan, who was a tailor from Gloucester. Mr Jordan visited towns on his way to Newnham, before crossing by ferry to measure people for clothes in Arlingham, Frampton and Saul. His grandmother, Catherine Ballinger before her marriage, used to go to Brightlands as a boarder and went home on the ferry at weekends.

For the people of Newnham the ferry was used mainly for pleasurable pursuits, but for the Arlingham inhabitants it was a necessity. Fruit-growing,

The New Inn, under flood, Arlingham, early 1960s

fishing, farming, and weaving in earlier years, wei
Arlingham, so people had to cross over by ferry t
their shopping. They had to shout to the ferryman
and the fare was one penny for a single or twopence

There were many moles at Lower Milton End F
Blade, known as 'The Want Man', would travel to A
them. Cider was made at the farm and sold to the fre
Eastington, but the eating and dessert plums were tak
ferry and on to Grange Court, where Mr Phil Wooc
putting them on trains to sell in South Wales.

Horses, cows and sheep were ferried to Newnha
and were then sent by train to Monmouth and Abergavenny. On one return
journey a bull, 'Pincher' by name, was taken down the slipway to The Ferry
at Newnham and had blinkers put on before the journey so that he would
not know where he was going! The blinkers are still in Mr Turner's
possession. Members of the Hill and Hart families would take their horses
over to Arlingham on the ferry to ride with the Berkeley hunt.

The *Citizen* newspapers were sent to Newnham from Gloucester by train,
and were then ferried across to Arlingham, where local boys collected them
and picked up meat from Mr Price, the Newnham butcher, at the same time.

A letter was printed in the *Arlingham Church and Parish News* in April 1992
from Doug Aldridge of Bristol, in which he described the Severn as 'a
beautiful river' which, with the Bristol Channel ports, provided a living for
him, his grandfather and others for many years, and in which he swam during
summer months. He continues:

> As regards The Ferry, I was on the *Camborne* with Captn. Shaw, my uncle,
> and we moored at Lydney to load coal for Youghal in Southern Ireland, as
> it was the weekend we came home via Newnham and The Ferry. As we
> got to the boat two ladies wanted to cross, as they wanted to visit
> Arlingham Churchyard where they had relations buried. On coming on
> the Arlingham side, Uncle and I took our shoes and socks off and poor
> Tom carried the first lady across, goes back for the other lady and she slips
> off his back into the water. It was a funny sight. She went to the New Inn
> and dried out. I think Mr. King was there then. Whether she finished the
> journey I don't know, but as everyone knows . . . the river must be treated
> with respect.

Henry Withers, the editor, referred to this letter and a previous one
written by Mrs Gillian Tomlinson of Weston-Super-Mare (Tom Phillips's
granddaughter) in the same edition. He wrote:

Schoolchildren about to cross from Arlingham to Newnham, 1984. Left to right: Linda Doyle, Matthew Morrett, Catherine Downs, Edward Burcher, Thomas Burcher. (Photograph courtesy of Mrs Ann Burcher of Arlingham)

There's not many in the village who can remember him, only those over 80 and who have always lived in the village, people like Rennie Price, Charlie Greenway, Bert Wright. I'm 77 and I can just remember him carrying me as a small child through the mud to his boat. What I went to Newnham for I know not.

Continuing in the same volume of the *Arlingham Church and Parish News*, Henry wrote:

A vetenery Surgen by the name of Mashele lived at Newnham and attended most of the farms in Arlingham, crossed the river by Tom Phillips Baot and then hired a pony and trap from Bert King of Passage Farm and pub to convey him up to the village and to the appropreate farm, this only ceased about 1930 when Motor Cars became more prevelent and vets came from Gloucester and Stroud. Tom Margesson from Stroud was employed by the Ministry of Agriculture to inspect all cattle paying particular attention to udders for T.B. Now ours can be tested for T.B. regularly and any found infested are put down.

CHAPTER THIRTEEN

Tragedies and Near-tragedies

A former vicar of Arlingham, Thomas H. Ravenhill, wrote an article called 'Parish Registers of Arlingham', which was published in *Gloucestershire Notes and Queries* in 1881. This referred to the dangers of the river and, in particular, recorded an incident in 1644 when 'seventeen soldiers were drowned . . . being cast away in a little oar boate, and overturned by the violence of the waves of the flowing tide'. Five of the seventeen were buried at Arlingham.

Parish registers at Awre also refer to many tragedies and St Andrew's church, which dates from the early nineteenth century, has an enormous dug-out chest used for laying out bodies recovered from the river. In 1731 an entry records how the Newnham trow 'struck upon the sands above Amity Crib, the owner and seventeen passengers drowning and only four escaping in a small boat'.

The following extract appeared in the *Gloucester Journal* on 6 February 1809:

On Thursday morning between seven and eight o'clock, the passage boat which plies upon the Severn at Newnham, was swamped and sunk, when Mr. Hewlett of Frampton and the two boatmen were drowned, in view of several spectators on both sides of the river, who, although they instantly put off in another boat, were not in time to render them any assistance.

They had gone over to the opposite shore in the small boat, and were returning to Newnham to avoid the flood, when they were unexpectedly overtaken by the bore, or head of the tide, which set in with unparalleled height and rapidity, and were suddenly engulphed in the tremendous deluge, whilst piteously imploring assistance from the shore. When they saw that they could not escape the tide, they judiciously placed the boat end-on, but such was the overwhelming power of the torrent, that their feeble bark was incapable of resisting its awful force.

One of the boatmen, Thomas Knight, (who had been a faithful and cautious servant at that ferry for eighteen years) has left a family of seven children; the other, Thomas Rooke, has left three small children, and each of them a pregnant widow, in such circumstances of distress as to render them great objects of charity. Mr. Hewlett (the passenger) had been married but a few weeks.

Tom Phillips (left) and Mr Knight

In the churchyard at Arlingham one tombstone marks a collison between boats in August 1848. The inscription reads:

> Four youthful friends that fated boat contained,
> But two alone in life the shore regained

Three sons of the Phillips family of Arlingham lost their lives through drowning. Elijah Rowles Phillips was drowned in the Severn on 21 July 1855 at the age of fifteen. He was the son of Charles and Charlotta Phillips and was buried at Arlingham. On the headstone are the names of Lewis Phillips, drowned on 15 June 1875 aged twenty-nine, and Hubert Phillips, drowned on 14 August aged forty-three. They may have drowned at sea since the parish registers show that neither was buried in Arlingham.

On 29 August 1848 the Reverend John Lloyd Crawley, Vicar of Arlingham (the son of Reverend John Lloyd Crawley of Stowe, Northamptonshire, and grandson of Sir Thomas Crawley-Boevey of Flaxley Abbey, Gloucester), was drowned at the age of forty. The accident was reported in the *Gloucester Journal* on 2 September of that year. Revd Crawley was returning from the Forest of Dean

> at a late hour on Tuesday night, and not finding a boat waiting for him as he expected, he rashly attempted to cross the Severn on horseback. the tide not having run down sufficiently, and there being a considerable fresh in the river, he unfortunately lost his life in the attempt.

There was a follow-up article in the same newspaper on 9 September 1848:

We briefly stated last week that the Rev. J.L. Crawley, Vicar of Arlingham, in this county, was drowned on the night of the 29th ult. in rashly attempting to cross with his horse at a ford near Newnham, when the river was in a dangerous state from flood and tide. The body of the reverend gentleman was found about mid-day on Wednesday, nearly opposite the Box Cliff, a short distance below Newnham, and an inquest was held on the following day before John G. Ball Esq. of Stroud, and a respectable jury, H.C. Clifford Esq. and several of the neighbouring clergy and gentry being present. – John Hart, waterman of Arlingham, proved the finding of the body. – Thomas Watts Esq., surgeon, of Frampton-on-Severn, proved marks of injury on the face and temple, as if from the kick of a horse. – Mr. Karn, of Newnham, and Mr. Dowding, of Westbury, proved the anxiety of the deceased to return home, and his disappointment at not finding the owner of a private boat from the other side of the river in waiting for him as he had expected; that the deceased and another person

Sailing round The Nab, *c.* 1900

Horse boat entering Newnham Pill on the Gloucester side of The Ferry, *c.* 1900. The boat was loaded with bundles of withy sticks for making baskets and salmon putts (or putcheons). The boat arrived at high water

went in search of him; and also that the deceased rode down to the slip at Newnham, and into the river, in the proper direction of the ford, where he and others frequently crossed at low water; and also that receiving no answer to their repeated calls, they crossed the river in a small boat and proceeded to Arlingham, where they found the horse near the house of the deceased, and that one stirrup and stirrup leather were missing. – The owner of the private boat proved that he went for the purpose of meeting Mr. Crawley by appointment, and waited a considerable time, but then returned home, it being late, without mentioning to any one that he was about to do so; and that he had on previous occasions fetched Mr. Crawley in his boat when The Ferryman could not take him. It was further proved that according to the custom of The Ferry, and in the then state of the tide, it would have been impossible for The Ferryman to have taken him over and been prepared for the passing of the public in the morning. – The jury returned a verdict that the deceased was accidentally drowned.

A tombstone in Newnham churchyard bears the following inscription:

In affectionate remembrance of
Henry Brace
Aged 18 years
He was accidentally drowned June 28th, 1866

Gaius and Victor Phillips, the sons of Tom Phillips The Ferryman, drowned on 17 July 1889 aged seven and nine respectively. An entry by the headmaster in the Newnham School Records and Log Book for 1889 states:

> they were at school in the morning, and they took their father's lunch to him at The Ferry, which they did each day. Whilst he was having his lunch they took off their shoes and stockings and went to paddle. The younger boy got into difficulties and the other brother went to help him. By the time their father saw they were both in difficulties, the tide had taken them both away, and they were drowned.

Newspaper coverage of the incident (source unknown) is reproduced below:

BATHING FATALITY AT NEWNHAM.

TWO BROTHERS DROWNED.

A sad case of accidental drowning took place on Monday afternoon in the River Severn at Newnham. A number of boys from the National School have been in the habit of bathing and paddling on the sand banks and shallow of the river during the mid-day interval of their school. Two little fellows, brothers, named Victor and Gaius Phillips were engaged in the latter occupation, with their shoes and stockings off and trousers turned up, about 1 o'clock on Monday, when the youngest, aged 7, slipped off the shallow sand bank into deep water. His brother, aged 9, courageously plunged in to his assistance, but both disappeared after a short struggle, and were seen no more alive. The father, who is the well-known Newnham ferryman, was engaged in bringing passengers from the Arlingham side, in his boat, and seeing something of the accident, he hastened to the spot, but by the time he arrived nothing could be seen of the lads. By feeling about with a boat hook, it was not long before the body of the youngest boy was recovered, but although Mr. T. Knight of Newnham, and Mr. W. Crawshay of Hyde (who happened to be at hand) made every exertion to resuscitate the lad by the usual means, it was without success. Just then the flood tide began to flow, and the second body could not be found for some time, but by the use of drags it was ultimately recovered at 3 o'clock close to the same spot, life being, of course, quite extinct. Much sympathy is felt for the father who is well known and highly respected by the numbers of passengers who use The Ferry at which he has been employed for the last ten or twelve years.

THE INQUEST.

A WARNING TO BOYS.

Mr. M.F. Carter, coroner, and a jury of whom Mr. T.B. Fox was foreman, held an enquiry at the Police-station, Newnham, on Wednesday, touching the deaths of Victor Thomas Phillips (9) and Reginald Gaius Phillips (8), sons of Thomas Phillips, of Preece's-alley, Newnham, the keeper of The Ferry between Newnham and Arlingham on the River Severn.

Thomas Phillips deposed that his sons and another boy came to The Ferry. He took a passenger to Bollow, and on his return he observed that three boys were paddling in the water, and had got about 50 yards out from the shore. He did not recognise that they were the same boys as he left on shore. Immediately afterwards witness saw that two of the boys were struggling in the water, and he rowed to them as hard as he could, but they were out of sight and were drowned before he reached the spot. On pulling ashore, where Trenfield stood, the lad told witness that the two boys who were drowned were his sons. There was seven feet of water at the spot before flood; they went suddenly from shallow to deep water.

The Severn, Newnham, *c.* 1910

The Severn, near Bullo, *c.* 1920

Albert Trenfield (8), son of William Trenfield, the Bullo engine-shed foreman, deposed that the first of the boys to get out of his depth was Reginald Phillips, who cried to his brother for help. Throwing his boots and stockings on to the sand he rushed into the water after him. He got near and took hold of him and tried to drag him back, but they had now both got into deep water. They all cried out for help, but there was no one near except The Ferryman. When the deceased went under water he did not see them again.

P.C. Jackson having given evidence of the recovery of the bodies, the Coroner, addressing the jury, said this was a sad and very simple story, and he hoped it would be a warning to the rest of the boys of the town. He suggested that in their verdict the jury should distinguish between the two boys: Reginald having first got out of his depth, his elder brother sacrificed his life in an ineffectual attempt to save him.

The jury concurred and found their verdict as Mr. Carter had suggested. They gave their fees to the father, and we learn that an appeal which has been instituted has met with a very liberal response.

Mr. Preece, representing the owner of The Ferry, asked if the National School master would be kind enough to warn the boys. Some two years ago Mr. Dawe did so with satisfactory results. They had forgotten that warning, however, and if he would kindly repeat it it might have some effect.

Mr. Dawe said he would do so. He had already done so this week, but it was the parents particularly who should look into this matter, because such power as he had was only of a moral nature.

The Coroner observed that he purposed asking their vicar, at the funeral of the deceased boys, to allow the children to attend the service, and to address a few words to them appropriate to the occasion.

Another tombstone in Newnham churchyard reads: 'George T. Widdows who was drowned August 12th 1892, aged 13 years.'

A near-tragedy occurred when Ethel Withers, aged ten, who lived at Broadoak, was paddling near to The Ferry many years ago. As the tide turned she was stuck by the mud, but happily was rescued by friends. When she was older she married Harry Boughton and became the mother of Elsie Boughton of Newent.

A tragedy in the mid-1920s involved Mr Joe Bailey's horse. Before the slipway was built local people were allowed to put their ashes and waste in The Ferry area and Mr Bailey, who was also a carter for the railway, used to collect the rubbish. As he backed his horse down to the river one day he saw some children playing (near to where the car park is today) whom he thought were in danger. Mr Bailey called out loud, but the horse thought the command was for him and backed right into the river. The horse and cart were both swept away.

George James, the son of Bert James who lived at Cliff House, near to the Silver Fox Café today, was a member of St Peter's church choir, as was his father. When George was fifteen he went with his brother and friends to swim in the Severn, but was drawn into a whirlpool and swept away.

When Marjorie Dyke was about nine she came from Gloucester for her holidays to Newnham, staying with her aunt, Sophia Hooper of Church Road. One day while playing near The Ferry she became stuck in the mud and it took two men to dig her out and save her.

Thomas Parry, a Newnham stonemason, who died in 1936 aged thirty-nine and is buried in Newnham churchyard, rescued a schoolgirl from Cinderford (last name Middlecote) in 1932. He dragged her by her long red hair from the river near to The Ferry.

There are many similar stories of near-tragedies and of people being saved by the quick thinking of others nearby. One sad event, however, did not have a happy ending for the local Saunders family, who lived in a cottage in Newnham, known today as Windsor Cottage, at the end of the alley where Coronation Cottages are situated. In 1937 Mrs Saunders, who had her young baby Philip with her, sat on the bank by The Ferry to watch over her daughter Florence and her friends Elsie Parry, aged thirteen, and her sister Joan Parry, aged eleven, who were playing on the sands there. Elsie and Florence went into the river to swim. Florence, who could swim, was showing Elsie how to do the 'Dog's Paddle' when suddenly the current took both girls out to the centre of the river.

Bill Hayward, the ferryman, allowed schoolboys to play in his boat when it was not in use while it was anchored and on a long chain. That day Bernard Wheeler and Robin James were playing in the boat, and, hearing Joan calling from the shore, they pulled up the anchor and rowed out to rescue the two girls. One of the boys grabbed Elsie by the arms and saved her, and they gave an oar to Florence. The poor girl had been under the water twice, and as the oar was so slippery she could not hold on to it and was drowned. Florence's body was found at Broadoak a week later, and Elsie was a witness at the inquest.

In the Newnham School Records for 11 August 1937, the headmaster, W.L. Billings, wrote:

Florence Saunders, pupil of this school, was drowned today at Newnham Ferry. Elsie Parry, her companion, was saved from drowning by Robin James, present pupil, and Bernard Wheeler, past pupil. The Coroner – M.F. Carter – highly commended the gallantry of these two boys. The Headmaster had on many occasions warned the children of the dangers of the river: he had issued a special warning on the last day of term, 27th July.

The following is a copy of a letter the school received from HM's Coroner for the Forest of Dean:

Newnham, Glos.

3.9.37

Through the plucky conduct of Edward Robin James, the son of P.C. James of the Police Station in this town – and of Bernard William Wheeler a former scholar at the Church of England Schools here – there is no doubt that the life of the little girl Elsie May Parry was saved from drowning on the 11th August 1937 and but for the treacherous current in the River, the life of Florence Margaret Saunders would also have been saved by these two boys, who acted with courage and determination in their efforts to save her; it was indeed fortunate that they were not also drowned.

I desire to commend to you the conduct of Edward Robin James, and so far as my submission permits, to ask that some recognition may be given to this boy for his gallant efforts in this sad tragedy. I propose to communicate with the Royal Humane Society in this matter.

Yours very truly,

M.F. Carter

On the sands at The Ferry, *c.* 1920

Tim Wayman, who worked on the trows as a young man, was a great salmon fisherman. In the 1940s he was fishing at The Ferry area when he was caught by the tide. Fortunately he was able to slip his waders and swim ashore.

A man who took the *Citizen* newspapers to Arlingham by van used to swim in the river on very hot days. One day he jumped in to swim, went underneath the water and was never seen again.

On 2 July 1950, when Bob Whitney (now of Kingsmead, Newnham) was twenty-six and lived at Bullo, he saved an eleven- or twelve-year-old girl, Carol Passey (now Mrs Brice), from drowning. He was awarded the Royal Humane Society's scroll, which was presented to him by HRH the Duke of Gloucester on 12 September 1950 at the Old Court House, Littledean.

Another tragedy was averted in the 1960s when Mrs Hardy, who was newly married, and a Mr McKinley helped to rescue two children in the river. Mrs Hardy was commended and received a glass bowl in appreciation of her action. Both children survived.

On 13 August 1965, on his birthday, Keith Robert Pearkes of Newnham asked his mother if he could go swimming near The Ferry, with his Uncle

The White Hart, Broad Oak, from the Severn, *c.* 1920

Robert. Mrs Janet Pearkes, Keith's mother, refused, as he had just had a full dinner. His father, Kenneth Pearkes, then left to go to work on the 2–10 p.m. shift at the Bullo East signal-box. Keith then left home with Robert to go swimming, without Mrs Pearkes's knowledge.

At about 3.30 p.m. Mr Pearkes was busy in the signal-box, when he heard two men shouting out for Mr Perkins (meaning Mr Pearkes) in the fields below. At first he took little notice as he was busy, but when he realized the men were calling for him he got a relief for the box and went to the river bank, where the tragedy of Keith's death had already occurred. Mr Pearkes realized it was his son when he saw his brother, Robert, standing speechless by the river in his bathing costume. When Mrs Pearkes heard that her son was missing she thought he had gone over to the other side of the river and was hiding in bushes, but, sadly, this was not so.

There was an exceptionally low tide that day, and police divers, who went into the river roped together, said there was a deep hole near to the Nab, where it was thought Keith had drowned. Mr Everett and Mr 'Bob' Trigg also spent time in the water, trying to find the boy. Three days later Keith was found at Broadoak, near Pimlico Sands.

The force of the tide in the Severn was such that, in the late 1980s, two people who drowned at Lydney were washed ashore at a point near to Arlingham and Elmore Back.

Details of other known tragedies have been omitted so as not to distress relatives still living in Newnham.

CHAPTER FOURTEEN

Alternative Crossings

In 1810 there was a scheme for a tunnel to be built under the river near to Newnham. There was support for the scheme and excavations were carried out on the west bank of the river, in a field mid-way between Newnham church and Bullo Pill. However, the river water broke in on Friday 13 November 1812 and workers had a narrow escape from drowning. The damage could not be repaired and the scheme was abandoned.

The Gloucestershire County Records Office noted a scheme for bridging the river at Newnham in 1877. This was dropped owing to a lack of capital. The project was revived in 1880 but also failed barely before it had begun.

Fourteen years later Mr M.F. Carter formed a committee, with the Reverend Bevis, Rector of Arlingham, as his vice-chairman. Their meetings were held at the Victoria Hotel. This committee commissioned the firm of

The Severn Railway Bridge, crossing the Severn below Gloucester, c. 1910. The bridge was opened in 1879 and demolished in 1960

Keeling and Reichenbach to survey the river on 7 April 1894, with a view to
building a bridge, when observations were made to determine the velocity of
the tide. This was Keeling's last major civil engineering project. He died in
Cheltenham in 1913. The proposed bridge was intended to cross from
Church Road (Back Street), Newnham, to The New Inn at Arlingham, but
was shelved owing to a lack of financial help from the Gloucester County
Council, which was first constituted in 1889.

The Severn Bridge Railway (crossing the river below Gloucester) and
station were opened in October 1879. In October 1960 the piers on which
the bridge was built were badly damaged by a barge that missed Sharpness
Docks and came upstream, eventually colliding with the piers. William Hardy
of Newnham, whose knowledge of tidal conditions had been sought on
numerous occasions by British Railways, was employed by the Nordman
Construction Company as river adviser, and it was he who inspected the pier
stumps remaining in the channel after the collision. The Severn Bridge
Railway was demolished in 1960.

On 17 February 1939 it was publicly announced that the Old Passage
Ferry Company had acquired The Ferry rights at Newnham and intended to
establish a chain-ferry across the river. The Second World War intervened,
however, and the project was shelved.

Interest was revived in late 1948 when Enoch Williams announced in the
press that approval had been given for a crossing. However, he had become

The Severn Railway Bridge

The floating bridge, looking towards Arlingham, October 1948

The building of the floating bridge, looking towards Arlingham, October 1948

The floating bridge (made up of 'lily pads'), looking towards Newnham, October 1948

interested in Ronald Marsden Hamilton's idea of floating platforms, and the chain-ferry was abandoned in favour of a floating bridge. This was to be made up of hexagonal steel 'lily pads', each 6 feet wide and 30 inches deep, linked by loose bolting, which allowed the platform to move according to the state of the tide. These 'lily pads' had originally been designed for aircraft landing strips in the Pacific Theatre of war zones during the advance on Japan.

The planned route across the river from Newnham to Arlingham involved going down the slipway at Newnham, traversing the low-water channel by boat or vehicular ferry, and driving onto the floating bridge at Arlingham. However, the project failed as a result of problems of stability, with a loss to the company of £20,000.

A legacy of this scheme was the towing of the remaining 'lily pad' floats from Arlingham in 1956 to be utilized as a floating pier at St Pierre for Chepstow Yacht Club. Proposals were made at a later date for a structure that would withstand wind and tide, but nothing came of them.

CHAPTER FIFTEEN

Changes

In 1965 John Bellows, who was a printer in Gloucester, wrote about walks that could be taken in the Forest of Dean:

> Leaving Pleasant Stile, we can either drop down to Newnham Station in twenty minutes . . . or we may go down the road to Newnham. In this case, we should turn up the first path to the right after crossing over the railway tunnel. It brings us to a pretty little pleasure ground at the back of the Victoria Hotel, part of which was an ancient British Camp, or Outpost, for guarding The Ferry below.

Victoria Hotel, *c.* 1900. There were stables to the left (off the picture). The signs on the windows state: 'Smoking Room', Commercial Rooms' and 'Dining Room'

The Ferry, Newnham, *c.* 1896

Today the pleasure ground is known simply as The Green, with The Castle House adjoining and standing as a reminder of the old castle and earthworks site. There is no longer a station at Newnham, there is no longer a ferry, there is no longer a link with Arlingham – just memories, and always the river.

Appendix

The following entries have been included for additional information on names, places and terms referred to in the text.

Aldridge family
Harry Aldridge, who had a brother Ira, was the grandfather of Ron Aldridge, who now lives in Cinderford. Harry went to sea, as did his son Percy. Percy was the captain of the *Emily* in 1928.

The Bay
The Bay was a siding built to accommodate a steam engine and two carriages, which travelled from Newnham to Cinderford and from Cinderford to Gloucester. When the engine and carriages were waiting to go to Cinderford they were 'stabled' (a railway term) in The Bay.

Brigs
Brigs were brigantines – square rigged, vessels with two masts.

Crossings
There was a proposed Severn Crossing Bridge, prior to the Severn Bridge, opened in 1966. The proposed bridge scheme was turned down by a special committee on 12 May 1936. Percy Aldridge, with the tug *Benfleet*, carried out the survey in 1936, on which he was questioned for forty minutes by King's Counsel Craig Enderson. Sir Frederick Cripps, Chairman of the Gloucester County Council, congratulated Percy on the survey .

Finis
This trow, the best-known in Gloucester, was acquired in around 1920 by Captain William Trigg from Bullo Pill and Frank Boucher from Framilode to carry stone and coal. They worked it until it was laid up at Arlingham to maintain the river bank. The remains of *Finis* served as the foundation for a concrete machine-gun pill box during the Second World War.

Fish house

The fish house, below Unlawater House, is still standing and is today owned by the National Rivers Authority. The walkway to this fish house was known as Parks Wall or Perks (Pyrkes) Wharf. The quay was built by Mr Robert Perks, and wood was loaded from here to go Bristol. Collow, situated between Newnham and Bullo Dock, still has a fish house, which is used to store and box salmon.

Hawkins Pill

There was shipbuilding at Broadoak in 1802 at Awkins (later Hawkins) Pill. The Reverend John Pauncefoot Hawkins is mentioned in old deeds relating to 'The Bear Inn, Lands and Ferry 1827–1850', Ref. D.265 in Gloucester Records Office. The quay at Hawkins Pill continued in use from 1868 until early in the twentieth century. On 23 December 1868 Colemen and Mayo, of Hawkins Pill Shipping Quay, sold wood to the churchwardens of Newnham. Today there is still a Hawkins Lane at Broadoak.

Industries in Newnham

There was shipbuilding in Newnham from 1783 to 1794; ropemaking from 1858 to 1902, the business being owned by Mrs Elizabeth Clifford; and a reputed candleworks on The Green in the nineteenth century.

A detail from James Holl's picture of Newnham (see p. 11), showing the old Passage House or Bear Inn

Westbury-on-Severn, *c.* 1896

Karn, James

James Karn was an auctioneer who once kept The Bear Inn at Newnham.

Letters and statements regarding ferry fares

Kelly's Directory for the County of Gloucester and the City of Bristol for 1910 shows that George Sayer was a chief landowner at Arlingham and lived at Slowwe House. James Mynett Butt was a farmer at Court Farm and is buried in Arlingham churchyard. The same directory gives the Christian names of Captain Venner RN as Charles Edward Sidebottom.

By 1910 Henry Preece was not listed as a gent's outfitters at Newnham, but a farmer by the name of H. Preece lived at Woodside, Woolastone, Lydney.

Also of interest, the *Gloucester Journal* for 20 August 1904 stated that there had been a robbery at Henry Preece's outfitters shop, Newnham: 'underclothes, boots, shoes, caps, ties and stockings were taken'.

Ox boat ferry

The ox boat ferry was a boat specially adapted to transport cattle. The gunnel on one side was cut in order to take a wooden ramp and the boat was much bigger than that used to carry people.

Pill

Pill was the name given to the mouth of a stream and comes from the Welsh, *Pil*, meaning tidal creek.

Sayer family

The Sayer family lived at Slowwe House, Arlingham, but their main residence was at Pett Place, near Charing Heath, Kent. John Sayer, George's father, who died in 1886, was a lawyer.

Trows

Trows were the trading vessels used on the Severn, its estuary and tributaries since early times. The name 'trow' is connected with the Anglo-Saxon *trog* because of its trough-like shape. The first document to mention trows was in Parliament Rolls for 1411, but similar boats on a smaller scale were probably in use from Saxon times. Trows developed a distinctive shape and rig (the set of sails, number of masts, etc.) to meet local conditions. Built of oak from the Forest of Dean, they were originally quite small, with square sails.

Unlawater House

Unlawater House was known previously as Hill House, the home of James Wintle, and is today divided into flats. Since Lady Paget lived there it has

Unlawater House, *c.* 1908

been a children's home, a warehouse and in 1938 an hotel. Unlawater Hotel was owned by the father of Mr Peter Morgan (Wirral, Merseyside) from 1958 to 1962.

Venner family
Captain Venner's son, Major George E. Venner, was killed in the First World War. Miss Venner lived at The Reddings in 1919.

Wintle family
John Wintle was a trustee of the 1805 Act to amend and widen the road from The Ferry. James Wintle, who practised as a solicitor in Newnham from 1840 until a few years before his death in 1899, lived at Hill House. His trustees sold the house in 1908 and it became the home of Lady Walburga Paget, who renamed it Unlawater House. There was a firm called Wintle and Goodwin Chance, solicitors and commissioners for oaths, at High Street, Newnham, in 1910. In the same year John Wintle, Captain Maynard Francis Willoughby Colchester-Wemyss, JP, who lived at Broughtons, and Sir Thomas Hyde Crawley-Boevey of Flaxley Abbey were all listed as principal landowners of Westbury-on-Severn. M.F. Colchester-Wemyss was chairman of the Westbury-on-Severn Board of Guardians to the Poor Law Administration when Mr M.F. Carter was clerk, in 1903.

Flaxley Abbey, *c.* 1898

Newnham, before the clock tower was built, *c.* 1865. The Beeches children's home is centre right

Bibliography

Ayland, Norah, *Schooner Captain*, D. Bradford Barton, Truro, 1972.

Bellows, John, *A Week's Holiday in the Forest of Dean*, John Bellows, 1965.

Bund, J.W. Willis, *The Law Relating to the Salmon Fisheries of England and Wales with Statutes and Cases to November 1876.*

Clark, Leonard, *A Fool in the Forest*, Dobson Books, London, 1965.

Cooke, Arthur O., *The Forest of Dean*, Constable, London, 1913.

Dreghorn, William, *Geology Explained in the Forest of Dean and the Wye Valley*, David and Charles, Newton Abbot, 1967.

HMSO, *Forestry Commission Guide*, HMSO, London, 1974.

Clark, Leonard, 'Dear Wally', *Gloucester and Avon Life*, February 1981.

Hardwicke, Glyn, *Brightlands*, Merlin Books, Devon, 1982.

Herbert, N.M., 'The Newnham and London Traders', *Transactions of the Bristol and Cloucestershire Archaeological Society*, 1979.

Huxley, Ron, *The Rise and Fall of the Severn Bridge Railway, 1872–1970*, Alan Sutton, Gloucester, 1984.

Jordan, Christopher, *Severn Enterprise*, Arthur H. Stockwell, 1977.

Kelly's Directory for Gloucester and the City of Bristol, Smart, Gloucester, 1910.

Kissack, Kenneth, *The River Severn*, Dalton, Lavenham, 1982.

Mansfield, Canon R.J., *Forest Story*, Forest of Dean Newspapers, 1964.

Peel, J.H.B., *Portrait of the Severn*, Robert Hale, London, 1968.

Phelps, Humphrey, *The Forest of Dean*, Alan Sutton, Gloucester, 1982.

Rowbotham, F.W., *The Severn Bore*, David and Charles, Newton Abbot, 1983.

Verey, David, *Gloucestershire*, Faber & Faber, London, 1947.

Waters, Brian, *Severn Tide*, J.M. Dent, London, 1947.

Wood, G. Bernard, *Ferries and Ferrymen*, Cassell, London, 1969.

Woods, Mabel, *Newnham on Severn*, Albert E. Smith, Gloucester, 1962.